About This Issue Guide

The immigration issue affects virtually every American, directly or indirectly, often in deeply personal ways. This guide is designed to help people deliberate together about how we should approach the issue. The three options presented here reflect different ways of understanding what is at stake and force us to think about what matters most to us when we face difficult problems that involve all of us and that do not have perfect solutions.

The issue raises a number of difficult questions, and there are no easy answers:

- Should we strictly enforce the law and deport people who are here without permission, or would deporting millions of people outweigh their crime?

- Should we welcome more newcomers to build a more vibrant and diverse society, or does this pose too great a threat to national unity?

- Should we accept more of the growing numbers of refugees from war-torn regions, or should we avoid the risk of allowing in people whose backgrounds may not have been fully checked?

- Should our priority be to help immigrants assimilate into our distinctively American way of life, including learning English, or should we instead celebrate a growing mosaic of different peoples?

The concerns that underlie this issue are not confined to party affiliation, nor are they captured by labels like "conservative" or "liberal."

The research involved in developing the guide included interviews and conversations with Americans from all walks of life, as well as surveys of nonpartisan public-opinion research, subject-matter scans, and reviews of initial drafts by people with direct experience with the subject.

Coming to America

Who Should We Welcome, What Should We Do?

FOR CENTURIES, people from other countries have come to the United States in search of a better life. The steady influx of newcomers helped build America, creating a mix of cultures, religions, and ethnicities not found anywhere else in the world. Today, people born in another country make up around 13 percent of the US population.

As we begin to think about what kinds of changes we may want to make in our immigration policies, it's helpful to consider where we are now:

How many immigrants are coming into the United States?
Currently, the United States legally accepts around one million immigrants a year.

How do we choose who is admitted now?
Roughly two-thirds are admitted because they have family members already here. Of the remaining third, about half are admitted based on their job skills and half are refugees from

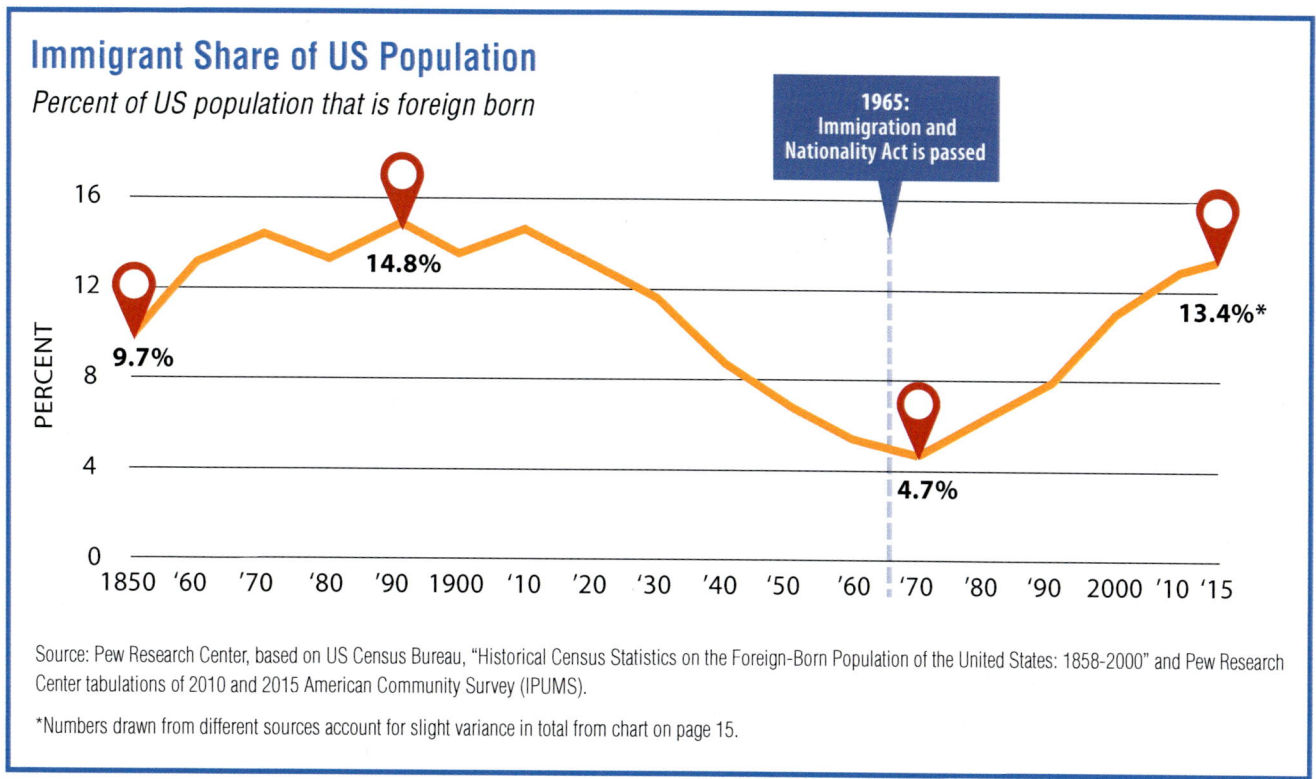

Immigrant Share of US Population
Percent of US population that is foreign born

1965: Immigration and Nationality Act is passed

14.8%

9.7%

13.4%*

4.7%

PERCENT

16

12

8

4

0

1850 '60 '70 '80 '90 1900 '10 '20 '30 '40 '50 '60 '70 '80 '90 2000 '10 '15

Source: Pew Research Center, based on US Census Bureau, "Historical Census Statistics on the Foreign-Born Population of the United States: 1858-2000" and Pew Research Center tabulations of 2010 and 2015 American Community Survey (IPUMS).

*Numbers drawn from different sources account for slight variance in total from chart on page 15.

political or religious persecution. There is a backlog of about 4 million people waiting to have their immigration applications evaluated and processed.

Has the rate of immigration increased?
In 1970, slightly less than 5 percent of the population was foreign-born. Today, the percentage has more than doubled to 13 percent.

How many undocumented immigrants live in the United States?
An estimated 11 million people now living in the United States entered without permission, typically crossing the border illegally or staying here after their visas have expired. Many have lived in the United States for decades, and have spouses and children who are US citizens.

Who are "the DREAMers"?
About 690,000 young people, sometimes known as "the DREAMers," were brought to the United States as children, many as infants or toddlers. A government program called Deferred Action for Childhood Arrivals

(DACA) granted them temporary legal status, but that program is now being re-evaluated.

But beneath these simple numbers is a maze of complicated quotas, shifting criteria, and unknowable timelines. Someone from a country with relatively few immigrants might wait 7 years for a green card, while a person from the Philippines or Mexico, which have millions of applicants, could wait 20 years.

Different groups of people may be particularly affected by changes in our approach to immigration:

- US citizens, including people born in the United States and those who have become citizens through naturalization;
- Newcomers who came to the country legally through our current system;
- Refugees escaping war or oppression;
- People now living in the United States who entered the country without documentation, many who arrived decades ago;
- People brought here as infants or children by parents who came into the country without permission.

Status of Immigrants Living in the United States

Foreign-born population estimates, 2015

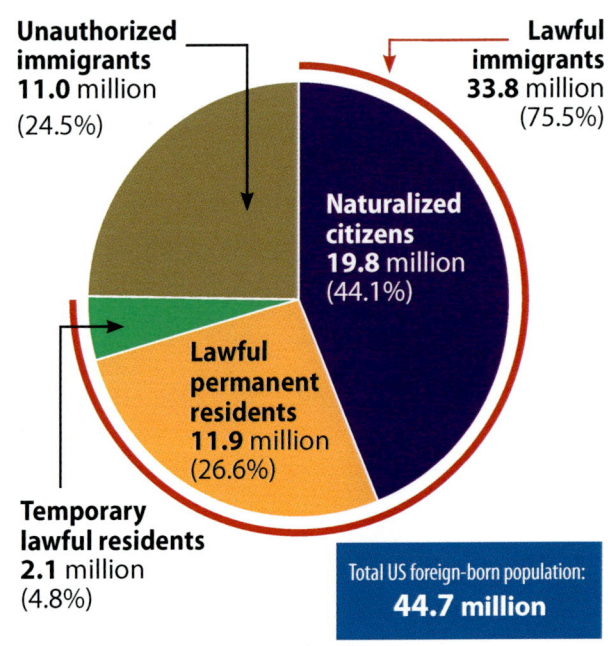

Unauthorized immigrants
11.0 million
(24.5%)

Lawful immigrants
33.8 million
(75.5%)

Naturalized citizens
19.8 million
(44.1%)

Lawful permanent residents
11.9 million
(26.6%)

Temporary lawful residents
2.1 million
(4.8%)

Total US foreign-born population:
44.7 million

Source: Pew Research Center estimates for 2015 based on augmented American Community Survey (IPUMS)

Refugees in the United States by Country of Origin

Number of refugees entering the United States in fiscal 2016, by origin country

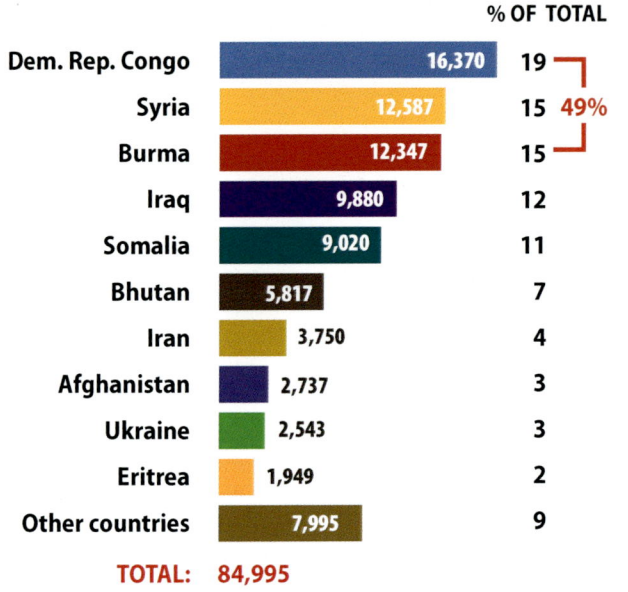

		% OF TOTAL
Dem. Rep. Congo	16,370	19
Syria	12,587	15	49%
Burma	12,347	15
Iraq	9,880	12
Somalia	9,020	11
Bhutan	5,817	7
Iran	3,750	4
Afghanistan	2,737	3
Ukraine	2,543	3
Eritrea	1,949	2
Other countries	7,995	9
TOTAL:	**84,995**	

Note: Data does not include special immigrant visas and certain humanitarian entrants.
Source: Pew Research Center, based on US State Department's Refugee Processing Center.

But the immigration issue affects all Americans in one way or another. American companies are experiencing a shortage of high-skilled professionals. Those out of work face increased competition for low-wage jobs. The news frequently reminds us of the threat of terrorism. And, while some communities are thriving with large immigrant populations, others question whether their communities will be able to assimilate the increasing number of newcomers. These and other challenges raise pressing questions about the nation's immigration policies:

■ Should we reduce the number of immigrants legally admitted into the United States each year? If so, how do we decide who should be accepted?

■ How should we handle undocumented immigrants in a way that is humane, but also fair to the millions who are waiting to enter legally?

■ Does the current flow of newcomers compromise our sense of national unity or instead build on a rich history of diversity?

■ Does the United States have a humanitarian responsibility to take in refugees whose lives are in danger? How many can we realistically accommodate?

This issue guide offers a framework for considering the priorities that should inform our nation's immigration laws. It presents three options for moving forward, each based on a different way of looking at the issue and each with a different set of prescriptions about what should be done.

None of these options are more "correct" than the others, and each option has trade-offs, risks, or drawbacks that need to be considered if we are to build a fair immigration system that reflects what we hold most valuable.

Option 1:
Welcome Immigrants, Be a Beacon of Freedom

THIS OPTION SAYS THAT IMMIGRATION HAS HELPED MAKE AMERICA WHAT IT IS TODAY— a dynamic and diverse culture, an engine of the global economy, and a beacon of freedom around the world. It says that part of what defines America as a nation is the opportunity for all to pursue the American dream. We should develop an immigration policy that builds on that tradition by welcoming newcomers, helping immigrant families stay together, and protecting those fleeing from war and oppression.

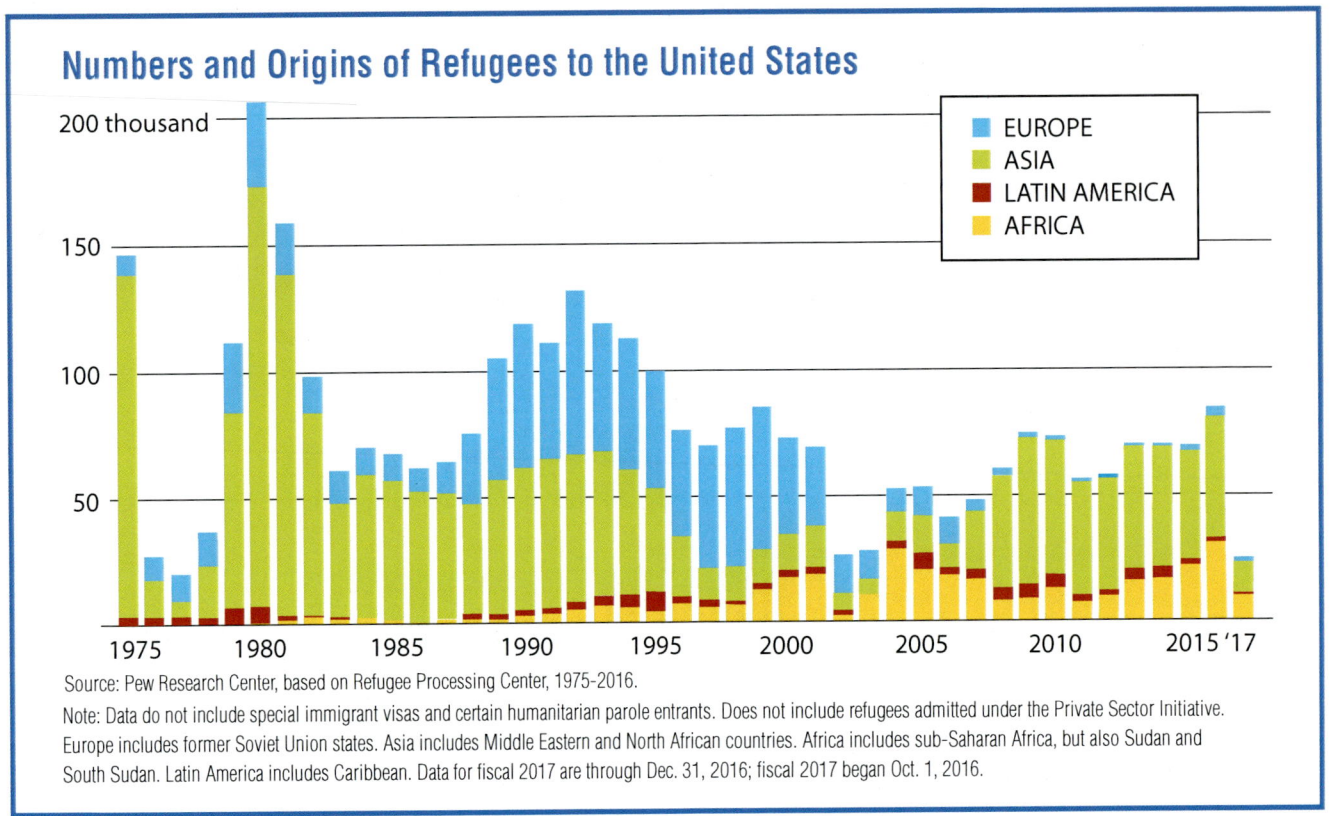

Numbers and Origins of Refugees to the United States

Legend:
- EUROPE
- ASIA
- LATIN AMERICA
- AFRICA

Y-axis: 200 thousand, 150, 100, 50

X-axis: 1975, 1980, 1985, 1990, 1995, 2000, 2005, 2010, 2015 '17

Source: Pew Research Center, based on Refugee Processing Center, 1975-2016.

Note: Data do not include special immigrant visas and certain humanitarian parole entrants. Does not include refugees admitted under the Private Sector Initiative. Europe includes former Soviet Union states. Asia includes Middle Eastern and North African countries. Africa includes sub-Saharan Africa, but also Sudan and South Sudan. Latin America includes Caribbean. Data for fiscal 2017 are through Dec. 31, 2016; fiscal 2017 began Oct. 1, 2016.

Welcoming immigrants is the right thing to do, according to this option, and it benefits our culture and our economy.

To remain competitive, we need newcomers who are willing to contribute their talents to strengthening America's culture of ingenuity and entrepreneurship, and who are willing to take on jobs, often tough back-breaking jobs, where there are shortages.

Historically, many of America's greatest innovations, like the scientific breakthroughs of Albert Einstein and the inventions of Alexander Graham Bell, were made by immigrants. This is no less true today. According to *Time* magazine, immigrants or their children, including Google's Sergey Brin and Tesla's Elon Musk, founded 40 percent of America's Fortune 500 companies. Untold millions of smaller businesses, the engines of American growth, were founded by immigrants.

Using US Census and Bureau of Labor Statistics information, the nonprofit group New American Economy found there were over 2.9 million foreign-born entrepreneurs in the United States, who generated $65.5 billion in business income in 2014. The immigrants who flourish in America do not just make a better life for themselves and their families;

studies show they generate employment opportunities, contribute to the well-being of communities, and have a positive effect on the US economy over the long run.

In some industries like farming, fishing, nursing, and construction, immigrants make up for workforce shortages that would otherwise compromise American productivity.

Visas and green cards are tightly regulated. Strict quotas and requirements exclude the vast majority of people who apply. And for those who do qualify, red tape and backlogs mean that applications often take years or even decades. The State Department reports that in 2016, there were 4.2 million people on family waiting lists and 107,479 waiting for work visas. Long wait times create problems not only for families, but also for American companies who need foreign workers in order to compete globally.

This option says we should honor our historical commitment to immigrants trying to reunite with their families and take part in America's unique culture of innovation and entrepreneurship. We have a humanitarian responsibility to people fleeing from war and persecution. And we need to create a path to citizenship for the millions of immigrants without legal status who already have deep roots in this country.

What We Should Do

Create a Path to Legalization for Undocumented Immigrants

This option says that we should create a pathway to citizenship for America's 11 million undocumented immigrants—that doing so will strengthen our communities, keep families together, and demonstrate our compassion as a nation.

According to the Pew Research Center, about two-thirds of undocumented adults have been in the country at least a decade. The vast majority must provide for their families and live their lives without the support systems that US citizens take for granted.

Some unauthorized immigrants work for cash and never fill out government payroll forms. But most have jobs and pay taxes on their wages, contributing billions of dollars to a system that offers them little or nothing in return. For example, the Social Security Administration estimates that in 2010 it collected around $13 billion in payroll taxes from undocumented immigrants. Under current laws, such people will not be entitled to any benefits when they retire.

The policies are especially tough for those brought to the United States as children. Sometimes referred to as "DREAMers," these young people have grown up and gone to school here, and typically see themselves as American. Some came with parents who entered the country illegally. Others came with parents who entered legally but overstayed their visa. They attend colleges, serve in the military, and own businesses. Yet many also live under constant fear that a deportation order will split their families apart and, for some, force them to return to countries they have no memory of.

There are a number of different proposals for providing a pathway to legal status for undocumented immigrants.

In 1986, President Reagan granted amnesty to about 3 million immigrants living in the United States without documentation. It was an unpopular decision at the time, but some argue now that this would be the most compassionate and practical action for us today. Others call for a clear pathway to legal status and citizenship, but one that asks immigrants to admit responsibility for breaking the law, pass background and criminal checks, pay penalties and any back taxes they owe, and meet other requirements.

This approach would be in sharp contrast to proposals that either call for high fines or so-called "touchback" provisions, requiring that people who are here without permission leave the country in order to return on a path to legal status. Given the backlogs and red tape, this would essentially be self-deportation. What we need instead, according to this

Seventh-grade teacher Kareli Lizárraga works with her students at STRIVE Prep in Denver, Colorado. She was brought to the United States without documentation as a 4-year-old, and became an educator thanks to the Deferred Action for Childhood Arrivals (DACA) program.

option, are rules that can bring people out of the shadows and into mainstream society so they can legally work and contribute to the common good.

Accept Immigrants Willing to Meet America's Workforce Needs

This option also says that we need to develop an immigration strategy that is responsive to the changing needs of the US economy, making it easier for people from other countries to come to America to work in industries where their talents are needed. We could do that by expanding the number of temporary work permits—H-1B visas—granted to high-skilled professionals. The United States issues only 65,000 of that type of visa each year, a small fraction of the total. This option says the limits should be substantially changed or even eliminated.

We should also, according to this option, offer green cards to foreign students who have earned graduate degrees from American colleges and universities—especially those in science, technology, engineering, and mathematics—to encourage them to stay in America and contribute to the US economy.

We could also create "start-up" visas for foreign entrepreneurs. A small number of visas are reserved for foreign investors, but this would increase the number and expand it to include patent holders, business managers, academic researchers, breakthrough scientists, and others with unique contributions to make in the 21st-century knowledge economy.

The US workforce also depends on less-skilled workers—those who can fill labor shortages in fields like agriculture, food preparation, and personal care. According to this option, we ought to create a temporary visa program that is adjusted annually depending on the current and upcoming needs of the US economy.

Accept More Refugees

Honoring America's historical commitment to immigrants also means offering refuge to people fleeing from war, conflict, and persecution. There are more people seeking political asylum than at any time in history, according to the United Nations.

The United States has traditionally granted citizenship to more refugees than any other country. Since 1982, the nation has accepted 69 percent of the total number of worldwide refugees that the United Nations has identified as eligible for resettlement, well ahead of the two other leading nations—Canada (14 percent) and Australia (11 percent).

The number of refugees brought into the United States varies substantially from year to year, based on the ebb and flow of foreign wars, famines, political persecutions, and other events. In recent years, however, the number of refugees admitted has declined in comparison to the swelling demand.

In March 2017, an executive order was issued that sharply reduced the number of refugees admitted annually. This option says that America has a humanitarian obligation to expand, or altogether eliminate, these restrictions. The number of refugees in the world dwarfs the number who are resettled, but this option holds that the United States must play a leadership role in this area.

Trade-Offs and Downsides

■ Creating a pathway to citizenship for unauthorized immigrants could have the effect of rewarding people who break the law. It would also be unfair to those who have pursued a legal route to obtaining a green card.

■ Accommodating more immigrants would make America more diverse and weaken our sense of national unity and common purpose.

■ With the difficulty of getting accurate background checks on people from war-torn countries, welcoming more immigrants could increase national security risks posed by terrorists and other criminals.

■ Providing support for immigrants and refugees could divert resources away from the millions of other vulnerable Americans who need help.

Questions for deliberation . . .

1 If we do not guard our borders and enforce our immigration laws strictly, will that tempt more people to come into the country illegally?

2 Many people born in the United States lack jobs and a good education. Should we pay more attention to their needs and potential, rather than focusing so much on helping people from other countries?

3 Should having family members already in the United States be an important basis for admitting new immigrants? How does this help our economy? Does this make us safer?

Option 2:
Enforce the Law, Be Fair to Those Who Follow the Rules

THIS OPTION SAYS WE NEED A FAIR SYSTEM, WHERE THE RULES ARE CLEAR AND, ABOVE ALL, ENFORCED. With an estimated 11 million people living in the country illegally, our current system is unjust and uncontrolled. In fairness to the long lines of people who are waiting to come to America legally, we must strengthen our commitment to border security, crack down on visa overstays, and introduce more stringent measures to deal with immigrants living here without authorization.

The United States was founded as "a nation of laws, not of men," in John Adams' famous words. Yet over the last quarter century, we have allowed millions of people to live and work in the United States illegally. According to the Pew Research Center, the number of unauthorized immigrants living in the United States has grown from 3.5 million in 1990 to 11 million in 2017, although rates have slowed in recent years.

Ever since the nation's first immigration policies were put into place, the premise has been that admitting newcomers should be done in an orderly way. That is why we must strengthen our commitment to border security, track down people who have overstayed their visas, and introduce more stringent measures to deal with immigrants living outside the law.

According to this option, the first responsibility of a sovereign nation is to control its borders and defend against external threats. It says that keeping the country safe means getting serious about border security—especially the 2,000-mile boundary between the United States and Mexico.

We must also step up enforcement of our immigration laws within the country. The Department of Homeland Security estimates that out of 45 million foreign travelers who arrived in the United States during 2015, more than 400,000 were still in the country after their travel and business visas had expired.

Unauthorized immigrants are excluded from nearly all federal assistance programs, with the exception of school meals and family nutrition programs. But even so, unauthorized immigrants can put a strain on the public purse, particularly at the state level. For example, about 40 percent of undocumented immigrants living in the United States have no health insurance, compared to 10 percent of US-born or naturalized citizens. Because public hospitals are required to provide emergency medical care to all people, regardless of immigration status, those expenses

Estimated Unauthorized Immigrant Population in the United States

In millions

*There is no stastically significant difference between the 2015 estimate and 2016 preliminary estimate.

Source: Pew Research Center estimates for 2005-2015 based on augmented American Community Survey data (IPUMS); for 2016 and 1995-2004 based on March Supplements of the Current Population Survey. Estimates for 1990 from Warren and Warren (2013).

are passed on to all of us in the form of higher health-care costs.

This option insists that we must eliminate what some call "sanctuary cities" and states. These are places where local authorities have said they will not comply with the federal government's rules that would deport people who are here illegally. According to the government's Immigration and Customs Enforcement (ICE) office, this is widespread. Cities like Baltimore, Philadelphia, Seattle, and others—as well as some states, including California and Connecticut—have policies to only cooperate with immigration authorities in limited circumstances. Some cities have gone further. Newark, New Jersey, for example, does not comply with ICE "detainers," which are orders to hold people in prison so they can be deported. And in other cases, law-enforcement officials have stated that they do not plan to cooperate with immigration officials. This option says we should crack down on "sanctuary cities" that refuse to cooperate with federal immigration agents seeking to locate and deport undocumented immigrants.

What We Should Do

Get Tough on Illegal Immigration

According to this option, the first step in addressing illegal immigration is to deport those who entered the country illegally or who have overstayed their visas. This is the only way to ensure that our immigration laws are respected and be fair to the millions of people from around the world who are applying to come here legally. We need an aggressive deportation strategy, one that sends home many, if not most, immigrants who are here without permission.

The nation's immigration courts are notoriously slow-moving, and immigrants slated for deportation sometimes wait years before their cases are reviewed by a judge. When the court notices arrive in the mail, people may ignore them or go into hiding. This option says we must overhaul the immigration courts and make them much more efficient.

Another important step is to enforce temporary visas. One way is by using technology, such as fingerprint scans, face-recognition, and other means, to track people who enter and exit the country. Congress called for a system like this in the wake of the 9-11 terrorist attacks. But with 45 million people visiting the country each year on tourist, student, and work visas, the logistical challenges of this "biometric tracking" were immense. To date, the system has only been implemented at a handful of airports and border crossings. According to this option, we should do what it takes to roll that out nationwide.

This option also says that police officers should be allowed to check people's immigration status if they have a reasonable suspicion that they are in the country illegally. To help make this easier, we should expand federal background-check programs that help state and local authorities access the immigration history of people who have committed crimes. And we should also eliminate so-called "sanctuary cities."

©DAVE EINSEL/STRINGER/GETTY IMAGES NEWS

The border wall runs several miles through a rural area east of Brownsville, Texas, serving to help control the flow of undocumented immigrants crossing the Rio Grande River from Mexico. Several places have wide gaps with no gates visible.

Tighten Security

This option says that any attempt to stop illegal immigration will fail unless it is backed up by strict border security. One way to do that is to build a wall along the almost 2,000-mile long United States-Mexico border. There are less than 600 miles of fences and walls already in place. Another is to beef up security at airports and border crossings. We should hire more patrol agents and customs officials at ports of entry to more thoroughly screen out potentially dangerous people at the border. New face-recognition technology and computer data systems could also help us screen for high-risk travelers.

We can also improve border security by streamlining so-called "expedited removals," which give legal authority to lower-level immigration officers to order undocumented immigrants to be deported without a hearing before a judge. These orders prohibit people who cross the border illegally from re-entering the country for a period of five years. This would help ensure that people do not apply for a green card and then enter the country illegally to live and work while the application is considered.

Punish Employers Who Hire Workers Without Legal Papers

This option insists that we must hold employers accountable if they hire workers who are here illegally, a law that is rarely enforced. In fields that depend heavily on immigrant workers, such as construction, hospitality, and agriculture, there is what seems to be only a casual approach to following the hiring rules. Undocumented workers can submit forged documents and employers can just accept them at face value, which is all they are required to do under the law.

If we are serious about cracking down on unauthorized immigration, says this option, we should require employers to use the federal government's E-Verify program, or a system like it. E-Verify is a database that certifies a person is eligible to work in the United States by looking at data from the Department of Homeland Security and the Social Security Administration. The program is voluntary in most states, but this option says that it should be mandatory.

Trade-Offs and Downsides

■ Deporting immigrants who are in the country illegally would tear apart families, hurt their employers, and fracture the communities in which they live.

■ Stepping up enforcement of immigration laws would drive a wedge between immigrants and law enforcement, and compromise public safety by discouraging witnesses from reporting crimes.

■ Cracking down on sanctuary cities undermines local authority, adds to a climate of fear, and drives away the many otherwise law-abiding immigrants who are contributing to society.

■ Prosecuting employers who hire workers without legal work permits could cause chaos in industries that rely heavily on immigrants, such as agriculture and construction.

Questions for deliberation . . .

1 Should we balance justice with mercy when it comes to people who entered the United States illegally many years ago? How serious a crime is it, after all? Is deportation really a fair punishment?

2 Identifying and deporting undocumented people will cost billions of dollars. Is this really one of the best ways to spend our tax dollars? How will this help our communities thrive and prosper?

3 Should communities with undocumented immigrants living peacefully and productively in their midst be able to protect them, without federal interference? Don't people living in so-called "sanctuary cities" know what is best for their own communities?

Option 3:
Slow Down and Rebuild Our Common Bonds

THIS OPTION RECOGNIZES THAT NEWCOMERS HAVE STRENGTHENED AMERICAN CULTURE IN THE PAST. But the current levels of immigration are so high, and the country is now so diverse, that we must regain our sense of national purpose and identity. We should have a measured immigration policy—one that reduces the rate of immigration and assists newcomers as they become part of the American community. We need to find ways to accommodate newcomers without compromising our sense of national unity.

A diversity of cultures is a hallmark of American society. We are a people created from many nations, races, and ethnicities. This is reflected in our national motto, *E Pluribus Unum*—"out of many, one." Originally, the phrase referred to the act of political union by which the colonies joined to form a sovereign state. It also aptly describes the enduring tension in America between our characteristic diversity and our sense of common identity.

The American naturalization ceremony expresses a two-way commitment. We agree to accept and welcome new immigrants as American citizens, with all the rights citizenship conveys, and the new citizens agree to become part of this culture, which is why new applicants are tested on their knowledge of the Constitution.

This option says that the current levels of immigration are so high, and the country is now so diverse, that we are losing our sense of shared purpose and national unity. As the late historian Arthur Schlesinger Jr. said, "We've got too much *pluribus* and not enough *unum*."

Over the last five decades, the immigrant population in the United States has expanded dramatically. In 1970, just 4.7 percent of the population was foreign-born. Today, the number is 13 percent. According to the Pew Research Center, the foreign-born population in the United States could reach 18 percent by 2065. This rise can be attributed in large part to the 1965 Immigration and Nationality Act, which increased not only the number, but also the diversity, of newcomers. The law eliminated the use of national-origin quotas and replaced it with a "family preference" system for lawful immigration. Today, family reunification accounts for two-thirds of new immigrants.

This option holds that such increased diversity can weaken the fabric of society and compromise our sense of common purpose. According to studies by Harvard political scientist Robert Putnam, people tend to be less charitable and trusting of each other when they perceive that large segments of the population do not look or talk like them. Increased diversity tends to reduce trust and cooperation, not only between different racial and ethnic groups, but also between people of the same race and ethnicity.

This option makes the case for a measured immigration policy that strengthens our common bonds. In practical terms, this means reducing the number of admissions, emphasizing integration, and making sure that we can accommodate newcomers without losing the shared values that define who we are as a people.

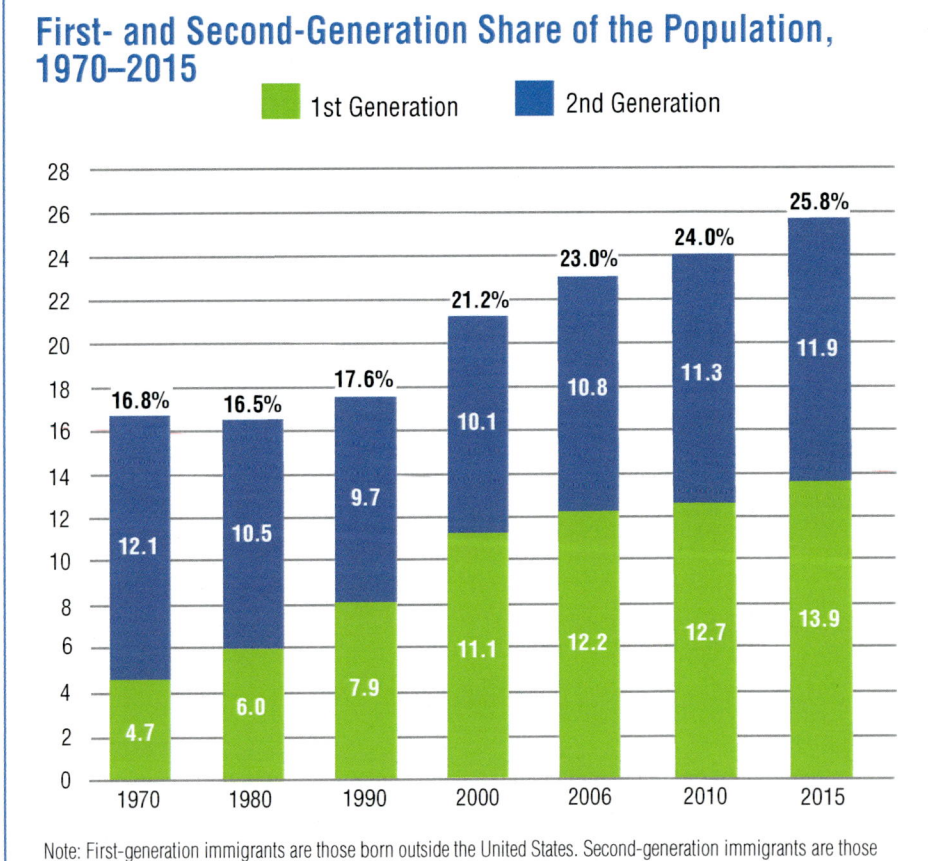

First- and Second-Generation Share of the Population, 1970–2015

■ 1st Generation ■ 2nd Generation

Note: First-generation immigrants are those born outside the United States. Second-generation immigrants are those born in the United States with at least one immigrant parent.
Source: 2000-2015 data and all second-generation data from Pew Research Center analysis of Current Population Surveys (IPUMS); historical trend from Passel and Cohn (2008) and Edmundsoton and Passel (1994).

What We Should Do

Restrict the Numbers of Immigrants Legally Admitted into the United States

The United States currently admits about 1 million people a year as legal immigrants. This option proposes that this number is too high, and that it strains our ability to welcome and absorb newcomers as we have in the past. There are a number of ways to reduce this number. Under the current law, US citizens can sponsor spouses, minor children, parents, siblings, and adult married children to enter the United States. Green-card holders who are not US citizens can also sponsor relatives, including spouses, minor children, and adult unmarried children.

This option says we should limit family-based immigration to spouses and young children. For example, a 2017 bill proposed by Senators Tom Cotton of Arkansas and David Perdue of Georgia would cut family-based admissions in half by doing exactly that.

This option also says we should eliminate the visa lottery, a program introduced in 1990 that offers citizens of countries with low immigration rates a chance to "win" a green card. The lottery confers 50,000 visas per year, or about 5 percent of total visas issued.

Strengthen the Integration of Newcomers into Their Communities

Another step we can take to reinforce our sense of common identity is to help people get established once they arrive from other countries. This is especially true in the case of refugees, who depend on placement agencies—nonprofits like the International Rescue Committee—to find new homes for them. While the agencies usually try to place people in communities where they have family or friends, many refugees simply settle in communities that are willing and able to take them in.

In 2016, for example, a quarter of all refugees arriving in America settled in one of three states—California, Texas, or New York. This uneven approach to resettlement means that many refugees remain in immigrant enclaves and never fully mix into American culture and society.

This option says immigration agencies should actively oversee the resettlement of new arrivals, making sure refugees are more evenly spread out and better integrated in their communities, rather than leaving it up to community organizations and nonprofits.

Some places have experimented with new and promising community approaches to helping immigrants get settled and become actively engaged in their communities. The benefits of these programs often extend beyond immigrants themselves to the community as a whole, resulting in new

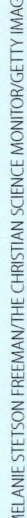
©MELANIE STETSON FREEMAN/THE CHRISTIAN SCIENCE MONITOR/GETTY IMAGES

Refugee Elizabeth Alier from South Sudan (right) works with volunteer Jessie Dotson on doll faces during an advanced sewing circle meeting, a Friends of Refugees program, in Clarkston, Georgia. The women in the group, who are from from Iraq, Bhutan, Burundi, Sudan, and South Sudan, sell their dolls and aprons on Etsy. Refugee resettlement programs have identified Clarkston as a good fit for displaced persons of many backgrounds.

jobs, economic development, and other positive outcomes. In Pittsburgh, for example, city leaders have created a program to attract "asylum artists"—individuals who encourage cross-cultural exchange and bring new vibrancy to older neighborhoods. Artists are provided with spaces to freely express themselves through public art displays, cultural events, and a journal publication.

Promote English as America's Common Language

This option recognizes that speaking a common language is a powerful unifying influence. Strengthening the role of English in American society and requiring that newcomers learn the language could go a long way toward integrating America's diverse immigrant communities. Current laws require people applying for US citizenship to demonstrate proficiency in English, but not those applying for green cards.

This option holds that we should give preference to immigrants who have learned English and make learning our language a requirement for lawful permanent residence here.

This may place a burden on some immigrants—refugees, for example—and hurt American employers who depend on foreign-born workers, but it would help newcomers thrive in our communities, join in our activities, and give them more opportunities and independence.

But there are additional steps we could take toward consolidating the role of English as America's common language. For instance, we could require that elected officials and government employees conduct all business in English. The intent would not be to ban other languages, but rather to foster and support the language all Americans share.

A further action along these lines would be to end bilingual school programs, which teach non-English-speaking children in their native language while they are learning English. While the practice is not as widespread today as it was in the 1980s and 1990s, many public schools continue to offer dual instruction in English and other languages, which is expensive and may hinder, rather than enhance, students' ability to become fluent English speakers.

Trade-Offs and Downsides

■ Restricting immigration might close the door to many of the workers, both low- and high-skilled, that America's economy needs to stay competitive.

■ Limiting the flow of lawful immigrants will split apart many immigrant families.

■ Emphasizing national unity and common identity will favor those in the majority and make it harder for racial, ethnic, and cultural minority groups to be accepted into the dominant culture.

■ Shifting our admissions policy to a merit-based system could hurt American workers by allowing employers to more easily hire high-skilled immigrants.

Questions for deliberation . . .

1 Is immigration really to blame for the loss of unity we see in our country today? Are there other factors that are more responsible?

2 Most immigrants are hard-working, family-oriented, and grateful to be in the United States. Will our communities really be better off with fewer of them? What will we lose if skilled, talented immigrants start going elsewhere?

3 Industries like agriculture and construction keep prices down by relying on low-wage immigrant workers. Will we accept the rising costs that come from paying higher salaries to US workers? Won't higher food and housing costs just make life harder for the working families in our communities?

Closing Reflections

ACTING ON THE IDEAS AND PROPOSALS presented here will bring about changes that affect all of us, in every city and town—those of us who are citizens and those of us who are not. It is important to think carefully about what matters most to us and what kinds of decisions and actions will enable our communities and country to thrive.

Before ending the forum, take some time to revisit some of the central questions this issue guide raises:

■ Should we strictly enforce the law and deport people who are here without permission, or would deporting millions of people outweigh their crime?

■ Should we welcome more newcomers to build a more vibrant and diverse society, or does this pose too great a threat to national unity?

■ Should we accept more of the growing numbers of refugees from war-torn regions, or should we avoid the risk of allowing in people whose backgrounds may not have been fully checked?

■ Should our priority be to help immigrants assimilate into our distinctively American way of life, including learning English, or should we instead celebrate a growing mosaic of different peoples?

Some important questions to consider are these: Where do we agree? Where do we need to talk more? Who else should we hear from? What more do we need to know? How do the ideas and options in this guide affect what we do as individuals, as members of our communities, and as citizens and residents in the United States as a whole?

Summary

Option 1:

Welcome Immigrants, Be a Beacon of Freedom

THIS OPTION SAYS THAT IMMIGRATION HAS HELPED MAKE AMERICA WHAT IT IS TODAY—a dynamic and diverse culture, an engine of the global economy, and a beacon of freedom around the world. We should develop an immigration policy that builds on that tradition, one that welcomes newcomers, helps immigrant families stay together, and protects those fleeing from war and oppression. Welcoming immigrants is not only the right thing to do; it benefits our culture and our economy. To remain competitive in a fast-changing global marketplace, the United States needs newcomers who are willing to contribute their talents to strengthening America's culture of ingenuity and entrepreneurship.

A Primary Drawback

This option would add even more burdens to systems that are already overwhelmed by historically high levels of immigration.

ACTIONS	DRAWBACKS
Give those who entered the US without permission years ago a path to legal status. It's time to forgive and welcome these people who have become part of our communities.	This allows immigrants who violated our laws to "cut in front" of the thousands of people who are seeking to enter the United States legally.
Welcome immigrants who are willing to work, whether in low-skilled jobs many Americans do not want, or in high-skill jobs where there are shortages.	Millions of Americans are unemployed. We should focus on the training needed to employ our own citizens.
Accept more refugees fleeing war and deprivation in countries like Syria. We have a moral obligation to help.	There are Americans in need too, and it is difficult to vet people coming from such war-torn areas.
Provide legal residency and the ability to apply for citizenship to undocumented immigrants who were brought to the United States as young children, sometimes called "DREAMers."	It's not fair to allow this group to benefit from the illegal actions of their families.
Allow all residents to vote in city elections, regardless of whether they are citizens or not.	This makes the word "citizen" meaningless.
What else?	What's the trade-off?

Option 2:

Enforce the Law, Be Fair to Those Who Follow the Rules

THIS OPTION SAYS WE NEED A FAIR SYSTEM, WHERE THE RULES ARE CLEAR AND, ABOVE ALL, ENFORCED. Ever since the nation's first immigration policies were put into place, the premise has been that welcoming newcomers should be done in an orderly way. But with an estimated 11 million people living in the country illegally, our current system is unjust and uncontrolled. In fairness to the long lines of people who are waiting to come to America and stay here legally, we have an obligation to enforce our borders and deport people who entered the country without our permission and vetting. That is why we must strengthen our commitment to border security, crack down on visa overstays, and introduce more stringent measures to deal with immigrants living outside the law.

A Primary Drawback

This will harm millions of people now living in our communities and contributing to our society. It will spread fear in cities and towns nationwide.

ACTIONS	DRAWBACKS
Identify people who entered the country illegally and deport them. Require that they reapply for entry.	This will tear families and communities apart. The punishment far outweighs the crime and is impractical.
Require police officers to check a person's immigration status if there is reasonable suspicion.	This hampers law enforcement by making immigrants afraid of reporting crimes and talking to police. It also leads to racial profiling.
Prosecute employers if they hire workers without legal papers.	This will create chaos in industries like agriculture and construction, and lead to higher prices for basic goods like food and housing.
Cut off federal funds to "sanctuary cities" that refuse to cooperate with federal immigration agents seeking to locate and deport undocumented immigrants.	This would undermine local authority and police, and drive away many immigrants who contribute to society.
Build a secure border wall, hire more patrol agents, and tighten security.	This will cost billions of tax dollars and fails to address problems with people entering from Canada, through airports, or people over-staying temporary visas. It will make it much more difficult for lawful travelers to enter the United States.
What else?	What's the trade-off?

Summary

Option 3:

Slow Down and Rebuild Our Common Bonds

THIS OPTION RECOGNIZES THAT NEWCOMERS HAVE STRENGTHENED AMERICAN CULTURE IN THE PAST. But the current levels of immigration are so high, and the country is now so diverse, that we must regain our sense of national purpose and identity. We need to moderate the flow of immigrants and focus more on assisting newcomers as they join American society. We should have a measured immigration policy—one that reduces the rate of immigration and ensures that immigrants become part of the American community. We need to find ways to accommodate newcomers without compromising our sense of national unity.

A Primary Drawback

This option would rob us of the energy and hard work people from around the world bring to the United States. In many cases, immigrants are more grateful for the freedoms and opportunities of this nation than the people who were born here.

ACTIONS	DRAWBACKS
Reduce the numbers of legal immigrants admitted to the United States each year.	This undermines the longtime image of the United States as a welcoming land of freedom, and deprives us of the workers needed in key industries like agriculture and construction.
Give preference to immigrants who already speak English.	This would place an undue burden on some immigrants—especially those who are willing to take on some of the back-breaking jobs most Americans do not want.
Restrict family reunification to spouses and young children, and concentrate on admitting immigrants who will work in areas where we need them.	This would split immigrant families apart, forcing people who come here to leave loved ones behind, sometimes in danger and poverty.
Rather than focusing on providing bilingual school programs, schools should ramp up efforts to help newcomers learn English and enhance curricular efforts to learn about American culture and democratic values.	Without bilingual education, students will be left at a disadvantage in today's global society.
Welcome refugees fleeing political and religious persecution while making sure they are not all resettled in the same place, which overburdens a community's ability to provide the help refugees need and makes it harder for refugees to become part of the larger community.	This would require more communities to accept and welcome newcomers.
What else?	**What's the trade-off?**

The National Issues Forums

The National Issues Forums (NIF) is a network of organizations that bring together citizens around the nation to talk about pressing social and political issues of the day. Thousands of community organizations, including schools, libraries, churches, civic groups, and others, have held forums designed to give people a public voice in the affairs of their communities and their nation.

Forum participants engage in deliberation, which is simply weighing options for action against things held commonly valuable. This calls upon them to listen respectfully to others, sort out their views in terms of what they most value, consider courses of action and their disadvantages, and seek to identify actionable areas of common ground.

Issue guides like this one are designed to frame and support these conversations. They present varying perspectives on the issue at hand, suggest actions to address identified problems, and note the trade-offs of taking those actions to remind participants that all solutions have costs as well as benefits.

In this way, forum participants move from holding individual opinions to making collective choices as members of a community—the kinds of choices from which public policy may be forged or public action may be taken, at community as well as national levels.

Forum Questionnaire

If you participated in this forum, please fill out a questionnaire, which is included in this issue guide or can be accessed online at **www.nifi.org/questionnaires**. If you are filling out the enclosed questionnaire, please return the completed form to your moderator or to the National Issues Forums Institute, 100 Commons Road, Dayton, Ohio 45459.

If you moderated this forum, please fill out a Moderator Response sheet, which is online at **www.nifi.org/questionnaires**.

Your responses play a vital role in providing information that is used to communicate your views to others, including officeholders, the media, and other citizens.